ASHANTI TO ZULU

PICTURES BY LEO AND DIANE DILLON

DIAL BOOKS FOR YOUNG READERS
E. P. DUTTON, INC. · NEW YORK

ASHANTI TO ZULU

AFRICAN TRADITIONS

· MARGARET MUSGROVE ·

To George and Gramma Holden

This book has been prepared with great concern for accuracy and detail. The author has lived and studied in Ghana and has done extensive research there, at the University of Massachusetts, and at Yale in order to write this book. In preparing their illustrations, the artists have done considerable further research, consulting numerous publications, The Schomburg Center for Research in Black Culture, the New York Public Library Picture Collection, the United Nations Library and Information Office, and the American Museum of Natural History. In order to show as much as possible about each different people, in most paintings they have included a man, a woman, a child, their living quarters, an artifact, and a local animal, though in some cases these different elements would not ordinarily be seen together. Every detail has been studied and rendered accurately, then interpretively drawn together with remarkable artistic insight.

The art for this book was prepared in pastels, watercolors, and acrylics. The frames that surround each picture were done in watercolor and black ink. The interwoven design at the corners of each frame is based on the Kano Knot, which symbolizes endless searching—a design originally used in the then-flourishing city of Kano in northern Nigeria during the sixteenth and seventeenth centuries.

Typography by Atha Tehon
Production by Warren Wallerstein
Separations by Rainbows Inc.
Printed by Holyoke Lithograph Co. Inc.
Binding by Economy Bookbinding Corp.

Library of Congress Cataloging in Publication Data
Musgrove, Margaret
Ashanti to Zulu: African Traditions
Summary: Explains some traditions and customs of
twenty-six African tribes beginning with the letters from A to Z.
1. Ethnology—Africa—Juvenile literature.
[1. Ethnology—Africa. 2. Africa—Social life and customs]
I. Dillon, Leo. II. Dillon, Diane. III. Title.
GN645.M87   960   76-6610
ISBN 0-8037-0357-0
ISBN 0-8037-0358-9 lib. bdg.

While a Kung boy searches for water under the desert sand and a Lozi girl settles into a boat to leave her flooded home, a Dogon farmer is carving his fields into a mountainside, and a Jie herder is grazing his cattle on flat green grasslands. As a Ouadai market woman bargains from beneath the shelter of woven leaves that protects her from the hot sun, a Xhosa woman wraps up in a blanket to keep warm.

This is Africa, an enormous and varied continent inhabited by hundreds of different peoples whose array of customs and traditions are as diverse as the land itself. In this collection of vignettes I have tried to introduce the reader to twenty-six African peoples by depicting a custom important to each. Some of the customs are unique and relate only to a particular people. Others are shared by many peoples, but all reflect African values or philosophies.

In spite of the fact that modern technology is bringing new ways and directions to African life, the traditions that have been passed from generation to generation are still respected and practiced. I hope that this collection will give the reader not only a feeling for the vastness of the African continent and the variety of her peoples but for the place that tradition holds at the very heart of African life.

In many African languages prefixes are added to denote the plural. For example, when more than one Ndaka person is referred to, the word BaNdaka is used. For the sake of simplicity I have used only the root words throughout.

MARGARET MUSGROVE
New Haven, Connecticut
1976

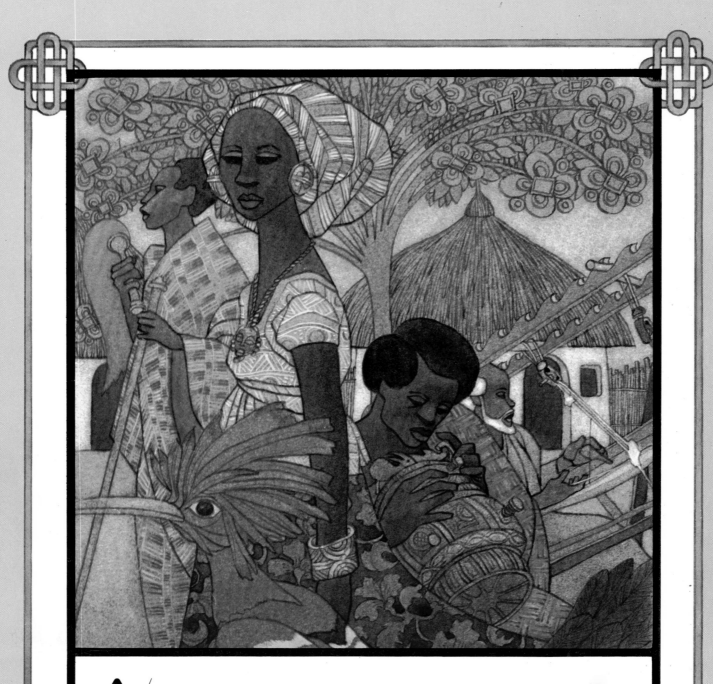

A/Ashanti (uh·shahnt⸱ee) weavers make a beautiful cloth called *kente*. They weave it in bright silk threads and give each different design a name. One, which is mostly yellow, is called "Gold Dust." Another, called "When the Queen Comes to Accra," is a favorite of many Ashanti women. "One Man Cannot Rule a Country" was designed especially for Ghana's first president. The Ashanti king drapes himself in a special *kente* that only he may wear.

B/To the Baule (bah′·oo·lay) a crocodile holding a big fish in its mouth is a sacred symbol. A Baule legend tells of a war with the Ashanti. The Ashanti had chased the Baule to a deep river. There was no bridge, so the Baule asked the crocodiles to help them across. The crocodiles agreed, but in return they demanded the most precious thing the Baule people had. Tearfully the queen gave them her only son. Then the crocodiles lined up side by side in the water, and the Baule walked across their backs to safety.

C/Chagga (chah´·guh) children grow up in groups with other children of the same age and sex. Often a group takes a name that sounds brave or proud. The children work, play, and go to school together. In a special initiation ceremony they all become adults at the same time. Chagga priests perform this ceremony in traditional costumes, and sometimes the children's faces are painted. After a big celebration the children are considered adults.

D/ The Dogon (daw·gawń) people are farmers. They live in Mali, where they carve their fields into the rugged mountains like wide flat stairsteps. Then they build stone walls to keep the steps from being washed away by rain or blown away by the wind.

E/Ewe (eh´·vay) drummers "talk" with drums. A long time ago Ewe drums sent news to people miles and miles away. Today there are telephones and telegraphs in Africa, but the drums still "talk." On special occasions the Ewe drum and dance together. The "talking" drums tell everyone what the dance is about and what steps to do. These drums have strings stretched from top to bottom all around them. By squeezing the strings against their bodies as they hit the drums, the drummers can make the "voices" higher or lower.

F/ The Fanti (fahn´·tee) offer their guests white bubbly palm wine that has a clean fresh smell. The wine comes from tree trunks, and the Fanti chop down or tap palm trees to get it. People sip it from gourds called calabashes. Before drinking, a person pours a little wine on the ground and says, "Come drink with us." This is called "pouring libation," and it is done to honor the ancestors.

G/Ga (gah) women make *foufou* by pounding boiled white yams with long thick sticks. This makes the hot yams smooth and pasty. Before eating it the family members roll the steamy *foufou* between their fingers and dip it into a stew. The whole family eats the *foufou* from the same bowl. It is Ga tradition to use only the right hand to touch food.

H/Hausa (how·suh) men are called to prayer five times each day. A strong voice rings out like a song, chanting "Allah is great" from the tower of a mosque. Allah is their god, and Islam is their religion. The mosque is their church. When they hear the call, Hausa men bow low in prayer.

I/The Ikoma (ik·oh´·muh) gather honey to eat and sell. There is a tiny bird in their land which loves honey but cannot get into the beehives. When this bird sees a person, it becomes excited and flies to him. Fluttering and chattering, it leads the way through the bush to a hive. The Ikoma always reward the bird with a gift of honeycomb — otherwise, they say, it may never help them find honey again.

J/ The Jie (jee´·yuh) are herders in the lovely green land of Uganda. The men spend most of their time roaming the land with their cattle while the women do the farming. Jie men love their animals so much that they name themselves after them. The animals are named for the colors and markings on their skins, and the men take these same names.

K/The short wiry Kung (koohng) people know where to find water under the desert sand and how to get it. They carry reeds in their skin bags. When they find a place where there is water, they push the reeds into the sand and slowly suck up the water. They store it in huge ostrich eggshells.

L/ The Lozi (low·zee) live by the Zambezi River. Every winter when it floods their land, they get into their boats and move to higher ground. First comes a black-and-white striped barge called the Nalikwanda. On it is a white cabin in which the Paramount Chief and the royal family ride. Boats of all sizes and shapes follow the chief's barge. Filled with people, stoves, and even cows, they move through the treetops and stilt houses to higher ground.

M/Masai (mah·sigh´) men groom their long thick hair with red clay and cow grease. Dozens of tiny neat braids flow over their strong lean shoulders. Pulled and looped into fancy styles, the braids flop heavily when they run or jump. It is Masai custom for the women to shave their heads and wear pounds and pounds of jewelry made of beaded iron and copper wire. They soothe the skin under the heavy wires with special leaves and grease.

N/Ndaka (n·dah´·kuh) people wrap a bride in so much cloth that no one knows how big she is. They circle her head with yards and yards of colorful material and make her a veil of sparkling clinking beads. Ndaka men lift her to their shoulders on a platform of young trees covered with flowers. A cloth stretched above her seat protects her from the hot sun. Flute players and singers dance gaily beside her as she rides to the groom's village.

O/A Ouadai (wah·dy′) market is held under leaf canopies. The sun is very hot, so palm leaves are woven together and stretched over sticks. Market women sit under these shelters and sell dates, meat, cloth, and other things. Their shrill voices call out as their hands and eyes beckon. Customers must bargain with them for fair prices. People shake their heads and walk away, but they come back. Bargaining is serious business, but it's a lot of fun too.

P/Pondo (pahn′·doe) boys love to spar with sticks. Each boy uses two sticks. He holds one in the middle and uses it to protect himself. He holds the other by the end and tries to hit his opponent with it. Moving rhythmically, the boys dodge and dart, trying to fool each other about where they will strike next. There is only one rule: A boy cannot hit his opponent's knuckles. The winner's prize is often the heart or liver of a freshly killed animal.

Q/Quimbande (keem·bahn´·deh) children can have as many as twenty-five brothers and sisters if their father can afford them. A wealthy Quimbande man can have many wives. Each wife lives with her children in a separate house in his compound. In the middle of the compound is a small yard where the women cook meals and the children play. The man visits the houses of his different wives on different nights.

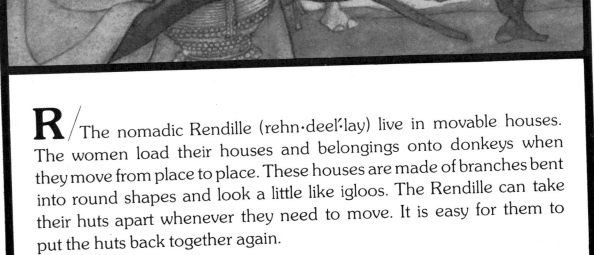

R/The nomadic Rendille (rehn·deel´·lay) live in movable houses. The women load their houses and belongings onto donkeys when they move from place to place. These houses are made of branches bent into round shapes and look a little like igloos. The Rendille can take their huts apart whenever they need to move. It is easy for them to put the huts back together again.

S/When a Sotho (soo´·too) girl marries, she does not carry a bouquet of flowers. She holds a magic beaded doll. The doll has no arms or legs, but it does have earrings. Its body is a bright beaded cone. It is Sotho custom for the bride to name the doll. Later, when she has her first baby, she gives this same name to her child.

T/A beautiful Tuareg (twah·reg) singer sits in front of a tent playing a musical instrument with one string. As the sun sets in the desert sky, she sings in a high voice while Tuareg men sit on the ground and pass around a bowl of milk. They lift their veils to sip. This is *ahal,* a Tuareg party. The Tuaregs are called "the people of the veil," but only the men wear veils. When *ahal* breaks into small groups, the women will do most of the talking. The men will peer over their veils, listening with great respect to the poetry and stories of the women.

U/Uge (oo´·gay) people collect kola nuts. The nuts are small and hard with pink shells. The Uge chew pieces of them like gum to keep from getting thirsty. After many years of chewing, their teeth become black. Kola nuts are offered to visitors as a sign of friendship and welcome, and priests use them in many important ceremonies.

V/The Vai (vy) people of Liberia carry almost everything on their heads. Men, women, and children hold their backs straight and their heads high to balance their loads. Some things that they carry are light, like cloth or small bowls. Other loads are so heavy and wide that a man needs help to get them on his head! Even women with babies on their backs balance heavy trays of food and huge basins of water on their heads. They move gracefully under these loads and almost never drop anything.

W/ Wagenia (wuh·gehn´·ee·uh) fishermen move carefully on catwalks above the dangerous rapids of the Congo River. Over a thousand different kinds of fish fill the river, some of them weighing three hundred pounds. The fishermen check to see if there are any fish in their giant handwoven bamboo traps. Some of the traps are ten feet wide at the mouth and fifteen feet long. It is the job of young Wagenia boys to clean and repair them.

X/ The Xhosa (koe´·suh) people in South Africa wear blankets to keep warm. The blankets are an orangy copper color, but they were white at first. The Xhosa rub a red earth called ochre into the white blankets to get the coppery color. Xhosa men and women are a striking sight wrapped in their copper blankets smoking their long pipes.

Y/Yoruba (yawr´·uh·buh) artists carve beautiful statues to honor mothers and children. One statue, called an *Ibeji,* celebrates the birth of twins. If one dies, the *Ibeji* takes his place and keeps the twins "together." Everything that is done to the living twin is done to the *Ibeji.*

Z/Leaping, bending, twisting Zulu (zoo´·loo) dancers salute their new chief. The earth trembles with the thunder of the drums as the dancers thrust their cowhide shields forward and wave their clubs. Their beaded headbands catch the sun. The furry white goatskin bands on their legs and arms move together, as if all the dancers were one person. The Zulus have beautiful and complicated dances for all occasions.

Text copyright © 2012 by Chris Wooding
Art copyright © 2012 by Cassandra Diaz

All rights reserved. Published by Graphix, an imprint of Scholastic Inc., *Publishers since 1920*. SCHOLASTIC, GRAPHIX, and associated logos are trademarks and/or registered trademarks of Scholastic Inc.

Library of Congress Cataloging-in-Publication Data Available

ISBN 978-0-545-25221-8 (hardcover)
ISBN 978-0-439-87759-6 (paperback)

10 9 8 7 6 5 4 3 2 1   12 13 14 15 16

Printed in Singapore 46

First edition, February 2012

Creative Director: David Saylor
Designed by Phil Falco
Lettering by John Green
Edited by Nick Eliopulos

PANDEMONIUM

by CHRIS WOODING
& CASSANDRA DIAZ

AN IMPRINT OF

SCHOLASTIC

NEW YORK TORONTO LONDON AUCKLAND SYDNEY MEXICO CITY NEW DELHI HONG KONG

9

SOMETIMES ALL I WANNA DO IS GET OUT OF THIS PLACE. . . .

THE MOUNTAINS ARE ALL I'VE EVER KNOWN. THEY SEEM TO GO ON FOREVER, BUT I KNOW THEY DON'T.

I'VE SEEN **MAPS**.

I COULD SPEND MY LIFE HERE. FIND A GIRL AND SETTLE DOWN. MAYBE BUY A FARM.

JUST **THINKING** IT MAKES ME FEEL EMPTY.

I'LL NEVER BE HAPPY HERE UNTIL I'VE SEEN WHAT'S OUT THERE.

DAD DOESN'T UNDERSTAND.

NOBODY BUT WE SIX CAN KNOW THE TRUTH.

YOUR DISGUISE MUST BE PERFECT.

YOU MUST DRESS LIKE HIM, SPEAK LIKE HIM, LIVE HIS LIFE.

WATCH IT, CHUCKLES.

YOU MUST FOOL HIS SISTERS, HIS SUBJECTS, EVEN HIS FIANCÉE, THE LADY ASPHYXIA.

FIANCÉE?

YOU'RE DROOLING, SEIFER.

SORRY. WHO'S THE CRONE?

BARONESS CRUSTACEA EFFLUVIA. SHE'S TO BE TALON'S MOTHER-IN-LAW.

SHE DOESN'T LOOK LIKE A BAD OLD STICK.

IT'S SAID THAT ONE OF HER MARATHON NAGGING SESSIONS DROVE HER LAST HUSBAND TO SNORT A BAG OF SCORPIONS.

AH.

ANYWAY, YOU WON'T HAVE TO WORRY ABOUT HER FOR A WHILE. THE BARONESS AND HER DAUGHTER ARE AT THEIR FAMILY RETREAT IN THE GLOOMDOCKS. NO TELLING WHEN THEY'LL BE BACK.

AND OF COURSE, IF OUR BELOVED PRINCE HAS BEEN KIDNAPPED, AS WE SUSPECT, THEN YOUR APPEARANCE WILL DRAW THE TRAITORS OUT OF HIDING.

GOOD OF YOU TO JOIN US, TALON.

I TAKE IT YOUR EGO HAS BEEN SOOTHED NOW?

THAT WAS WHAT IT WAS ABOUT, WASN'T IT? RUNNING AWAY FOR A MONTH, MAKING EVERYONE FRANTIC.

YOU ALWAYS DID LIKE TO KNOW YOU WERE IMPORTANT.

SUCH A CHILD.

I COULDN'T TELL YOU, SIS. IT WAS A SECRET DIPLOMATIC—

SPARE ME. AND WHY ARE YOU CALLING ME "SIS"?

REMEMBER WHAT I TOLD YOU. YOU'RE ACTING LIKE A COMMONER. ACT LIKE PRINCE TALON.

RIGHT, RIGHT. I REMEMBER. TREAT EVERYONE LIKE THEY'RE SOMETHING I STEPPED IN.

YES, THAT'S THE GIST.

I SUPPOSE YOU KNOW THAT THE ILLUMA ARE DEMANDING THAT WE HAND OVER OUR TERRITORIES IN RAVENFELL? THEY HAVEN'T SET FOOT IN THE DARKLING REALM FOR A CENTURY. YOU LEFT ME ALONE TO KEEP THE WOLVES FROM OUR BORDERS.

IT WOULDN'T HAVE GOTTEN THIS FAR IF YOU'D BEEN THERE.

STILL NEED ME TO HOLD YOUR HAND, SARCOMA? MAYBE YOU'RE NOT CUT OUT TO BE QUEEN AFTER ALL.

28

32

SQUUUEEEAK?

SHFFF SHFFF

HIS FAMILY, HIS FRIENDS, EVERYONE WAS LEFT BEHIND.

HIS PARENTS WILL GRIEVE. THEY'LL SEARCH FAR AND WIDE. THEY'LL WONDER WHAT HAS BECOME OF THEIR SON, OR IF HE'S EVEN ALIVE.

THEIR WORST FEAR IS THAT THEY'LL NEVER KNOW.

I WANTED TO LEAVE. I WANTED IT SO BADLY.

BUT NOT LIKE THIS.

I'M NOT FOOLING ANYONE. I'M NOT LIKE TALON, AND THEY ALL KNOW IT. EVEN THE CAT KNOWS IT. THEY HAD TO PRY HER JAWS WITH AN IRON BAR. MY HAIR STILL SMELLS LIKE TUNA.

THEY TOOK ME FROM MY HOME. THEY MADE ME A SHADOW.

HOW COULD THEY DO THAT?

PAF!

WHATCHA WRITING?

YAAAA!

39

45

WHOOMPH!

HEY!

HEY.

YOUR SISTER DID NOT TAKE SUCH AN UNREASONABLE STANCE ON THE MATTER, PRINCE TALON. SHE WAS PREPARED TO COMPROMISE.

MY SISTER IS NOT HERE, AMBASSADOR. YOU'RE DEALING WITH **ME** NOW.

LET'S GET DOWN TO BUSINESS, SHALL WE? YOU WANT RAVENFELL. THE DARKLINGS CONSIDER ANY ENCROACHMENT ON OUR LANDS AS AN ACT OF **WAR**. SO WHERE DO WE GO FROM HERE?

WE BOTH KNOW SARCOMA IS THE RULER OF THE DARKLINGS IN ALL BUT NAME SINCE OUR GRANDMOTHER, THE QUEEN, BECAME . . . CONFUSED.

BUT SHE KNOWS NOTHING OF WAR. WHEN IT COMES TO THE DEFENSE OF THE REALM, THE ARMIES LISTEN TO **ME**.

PERHAPS YOU DID NOT HEAR WHILE YOU WERE . . . INDISPOSED, PRINCE TALON. WE HAVE DISCOVERED ANCIENT SCROLLS THAT REVEAL THE LOCATION OF A RELIC SACRED TO OUR FAITH. IT WAS HIDDEN BY OUR PRIESTS BEFORE THEY WERE SLAUGHTERED BY THE DARKLING TRAITORS DURING THE POISONHEART REVOLT, A THOUSAND YEARS AGO.

YOU CALL US TRAITORS NOW, BUT YOU CALLED US **SLAVES** FOR A THOUSAND YEARS BEFORE THAT. ANYWAY, LET'S NOT ARGUE OVER THE PAST. WE BOTH KNOW THIS RELIC IS A FLIMSY EXCUSE FOR AN INVASION. THE ILLUMA HAVE NEVER STOPPED THINKING OF THE DARKLING LANDS AS THEIRS.

THE RELIC IS BURIED BENEATH RAVENFELL, PRINCE TALON. OUR GODS HAVE SHOWN US WHERE. THEY WILL NOT PERMIT US TO LEAVE IT THERE.

BOOM!

WHAT IN THE TWELVE TUMORS OF TUBERCULON WERE YOU **THINKING,** YOU MANIACAL LITTLE WRETCH? HOW **DARE** YOU RISK THE FATE OF THE REALM ON A PLOY LIKE THAT?

WHAP WHAP WHAP

PAF!

SNAP!

STOW IT, GRAMPS. I'VE HAD ENOUGH.

WHAT'S WITH YOU?

I'M PSYCHING UP. YOU'RE RUINING MY GROOVE, STANDING THERE.

THERE'S NO SPELL ON THE DOOR ANYMORE, YOU KNOW. IT ONLY WORKS ONCE. YOU WON'T GET ROASTED AGAIN.

IT'S NOT THE DOOR I'M WORRIED ABOUT.

AWWWW! ARE YOU AFRAID OF THE CAT?

OF COURSE I AM. SHE'S THREE TIMES MY SIZE AND SHE WANTS TO KILL ME.

BUT MOG-RA WOULDN'T HURT YOU. YOU TWO HAVE ALWAYS BEEN BEST FRIENDS.

BESIDES, SHE'S SUCH A CUTE LITTLE THING.

YOU HAVEN'T BEEN INSIDE HER MOUTH.

64

THE BARON CANASTA MALEFICA ISN'T MY **REAL** FATHER.

NO MATTER HOW MUCH THEY TRIED, HE AND THE BARONESS COULDN'T HAVE CHILDREN OF THEIR OWN.

HO, GENTS! ONCE AGAIN I REDUCE THY PALTRY PRIDE TO MUSH! SEE HOW THOUEST QUIVER AFORE MINE MIGHTY DISPLAY OF CARDSMANSHIP!

DOES HE **ALWAYS** TALK THAT WAY?

I HOPE NOT. I CAN'T UNDERSTAND A WORD HE SAYS.

I THINK HE WANTS TO PLAY AGAIN.

DARE THOUEST FACE ME IN ONE FINAL MATCH OF WITS? CANST THOU FACE THE CRUSHING SHAME OF BEING THRICE MASTERED BY MINE STAGGERING BRAIN?

WAS **THAT** WHAT THAT WAS? I THOUGHT HE WAS ASKING DIRECTIONS TO THE LAVATORIUM.

THE LANDS OF CLAN MALEFICA HAVE ALWAYS BEEN SMALL BUT FERTILE. WE MAKE OUR FORTUNE IN THE SHADEBERRY TRADE.

WHILE MY FATHER GAMBLES, MY MOTHER LOOKS AFTER THE INTERESTS OF OUR FAMILY. SHE IS A KIND MISTRESS. SHE TREATS THE SERFS WELL, AND THEY LOVE HER FOR IT.

FOR MANY YEARS WE PROSPERED IN PEACE.

BUT THEN THE **PLAGUE** CAME.

THE **BIG-FACE PLAGUE** STRIKES WITHOUT WARNING, SWELLING YOUR HEAD TO THREE TIMES NORMAL SIZE IN SECONDS.

IT SWEPT THROUGH OUR LANDS. THAT YEAR, THERE WAS NOBODY TO COLLECT THE SHADEBERRY HARVEST.

WE COULDN'T MAKE THE MUSTER FOR THE ARMY. WE WERE **SUPPOSED** TO PROVIDE FIFTY ABLE MEN, BUT WE DIDN'T EVEN HAVE **THAT**.

NATURALLY, DAD WASN'T WORRIED.

NOT UNTIL **YOU** SHOWED UP, ANYWAY.

UNDER YOUR AUTHORITY AS LORD DEFENDER OF THE REALM, YOU TOOK A **FIFTH** OF OUR LANDS FOR CLAN PANDEMONIUM IN RETRIBUTION.

THE FIFTH YOU CHOSE HAD ALL OUR BEST VINEYARDS IN IT.

MY FATHER **PLEADED** WITH YOU TO RECONSIDER. THE PLAGUE WAS PASSING AND OUR SERFS WOULD SOON BE ABLE TO WORK AGAIN, BUT WITHOUT OUR VINEYARDS WE WOULD BE **RUINED**.

YOU DIDN'T CARE.

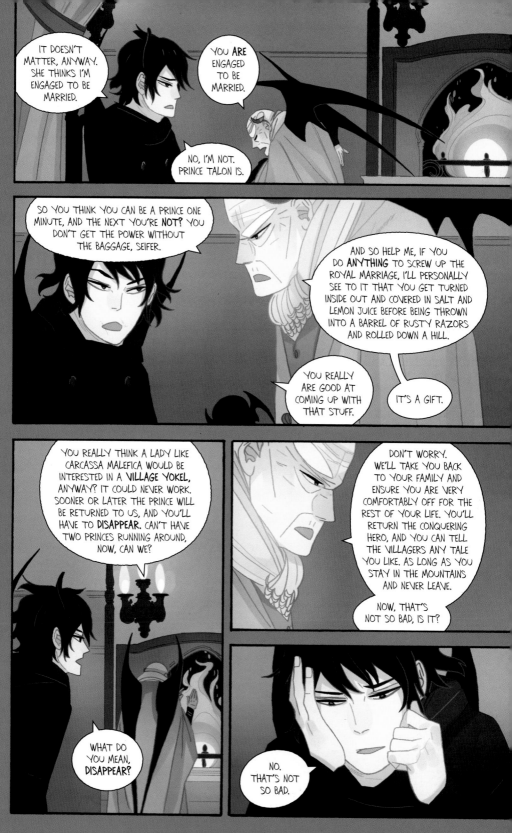

83

BE ASSURED, SEIFER, THAT NO EFFORT OR EXPENSE IS BEING SPARED IN THE SEARCH FOR OUR PRINCE.

OUR EXPLORERS ARE SEARCHING THROUGHOUT THE REALM—FROM THE MOST DISTANT MOUNTAIN PEAKS . . .

. . . TO THE BLACKEST DEPTHS OF OUR MOST FORBIDDING LAKES . . .

. . . EVEN TO FAR-FLUNG REALMS BEYOND THE **FRACTURES**.

BUT ALL THIS TIME THERE HAS BEEN NO WORD OF HIM. NO RANSOM DEMAND. NO CLUES. HE HAS SIMPLY . . . **GONE**.

Finest Silks

Finest Silks
HOT OFF THE SPINNERET

I HAVE A QUESTION.

YES?

WHAT HAPPENS IF HE **DOESN'T** COME BACK?

DON'T GET ANY IDEAS, SEIFER.

DON'T EVEN **THINK** IT.

THE HALL OF STATUES.

IN THIS ROOM ARE THE LIKENESSES OF THE HEROES AND VILLAINS OF DARKLING HISTORY.

THE MEN AND WOMEN WHO MADE A **DIFFERENCE,** FOR GOOD OR EVIL.

TP TP TP

CHIMERUS POISONHEART, WHO LED THE REVOLT THAT FREED THE DARKLINGS FROM SLAVERY UNDER THE ILLUMA.

THE PHILOSOPHER **EBOLA,** WHO FIRST THEORIZED THE EXISTENCE OF OTHER REALMS BESIDES OUR OWN, LIKE THE REALM OF THE ILLUMA.

HE EVEN WORKED OUT HOW TO OPEN THE FRACTURES—THE PORTALS THAT ALLOW US TO PASS BETWEEN THE REALMS.

THEN HE WENT MAD AND SPENT THE REST OF HIS LIFE TRYING TO EAT HIS OWN HEAD.

WONDER WHAT HAPPENED TO THAT ONE?

WHEN I'M GONE, WILL ANYONE EVEN KNOW I WAS HERE?

WILL ANYONE BUILD A STATUE OF SEIFER TOMBCHEWER?

BEARLOCK GREYCLAW.

I NEVER HEARD OF HIM.

I DOUBT IT.

SEVERAL NIGHTS AGO, THE VILLAGE OF SCARSDEEP WAS RANSACKED BY OLOG RAIDERS.

THEY STRUCK WITHOUT WARNING. NOT EVERYONE WAS FAST ENOUGH TO TAKE WING AND ESCAPE.

IN ADDITION TO TAKING FOOD AND SUPPLIES, THEY ALSO CAPTURED THE MAYOR'S SON.

THEN THEY DISAPPEARED INTO THE NIGHT.

. . . SO THEN I SAID I ALWAYS WANTED TO SEE AN OLOG, AND YOU HAVE TO TAKE ME, BECAUSE IT COULD BE DANGEROUS AND BECAUSE YOU WERE SO KIND TO MY FAMILY AND YOU SUCK AT NOT DYING IF WHAT HAPPENED IN THE CATACOMBS IS ANYTHING TO GO BY, OH PLEEEEEASE, AND THEN HE SAID . . .

I ONLY WENT TO SAY GOOD-BYE. I DIDN'T THINK SHE'D WANT TO COME ALONG.

. . . OH MY THERE IT IS THAT'S FANG WHERE THE CHIEFTAIN OF THE OLOGS LIVES I CAN'T WAIT TO MEET HIM I'M SO EXCITED EEEEEEEE!

YOU KNOW, THE PSYCHO CARNAGE BEASTS EAT GIRLS, TOO.

DON'T TEMPT ME.

96

100

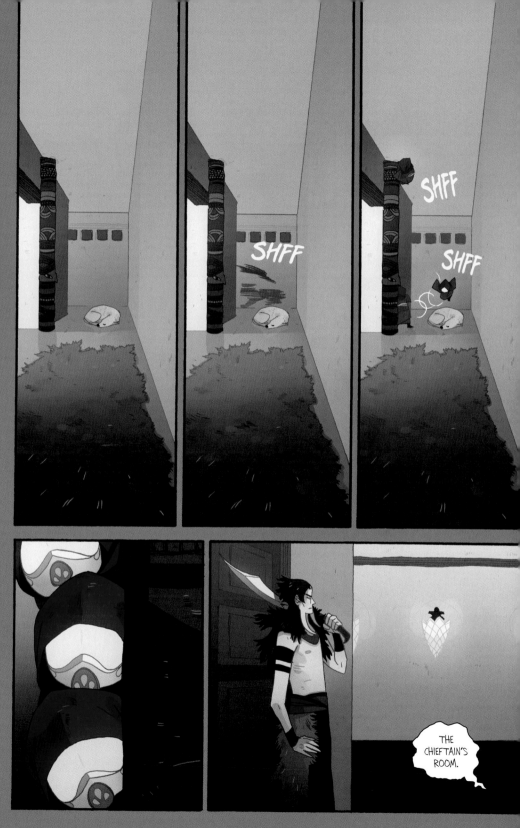

SHFF

SHFF

SHFF

THE CHIEFTAIN'S ROOM.

101

102

107

DAD, IF YOU EVER READ THIS, I WANT YOU TO KNOW THAT YOU WERE WRONG AND GRANDPA WAS RIGHT.

OUTSIDE THE MOUNTAINS THERE IS PAIN AND SORROW, BUT THERE ARE OTHER THINGS, TOO.

THINGS I WOULD NEVER HAVE FELT IF I STAYED AT HOME LIKE YOU WANTED.

I WOULDN'T HAVE MISSED IT FOR THE WORLD.

HOW IS IT POSSIBLE THAT I'M A MAGIKAR? MAGIKA IS AN **INHERITED** TALENT.

WHO'S BEEN KEEPING SECRETS FROM ME? YOU, DAD? MOM?

GRANDPA?

NAH.

I CAN'T DO THIS. IT'S ALL TOO MUCH FOR ME. I CAN'T THINK LIKE A PRINCE, A PERSON WHOSE EVERY CHOICE AFFECTS THE FATE OF THOUSANDS.

ALL I CAN DO IS WHAT I BELIEVE IS RIGHT.

MEEP.

ALL I CAN DO IS THINK LIKE SEIFER, A BOY FROM THE MOUNTAINS WHO KNOWS LESS ABOUT THE WORLD THAN MOST FIVE-YEAR-OLDS.

109

THOOM

WHOA!

CASSIE'S TRICKED ME OUT WITH A LITTLE MAGIKAL ASSISTANCE. IT'S A SLIM HOPE, BUT IT'S HOPE.

ANY CHANCE IS BETTER THAN NO CHANCE.

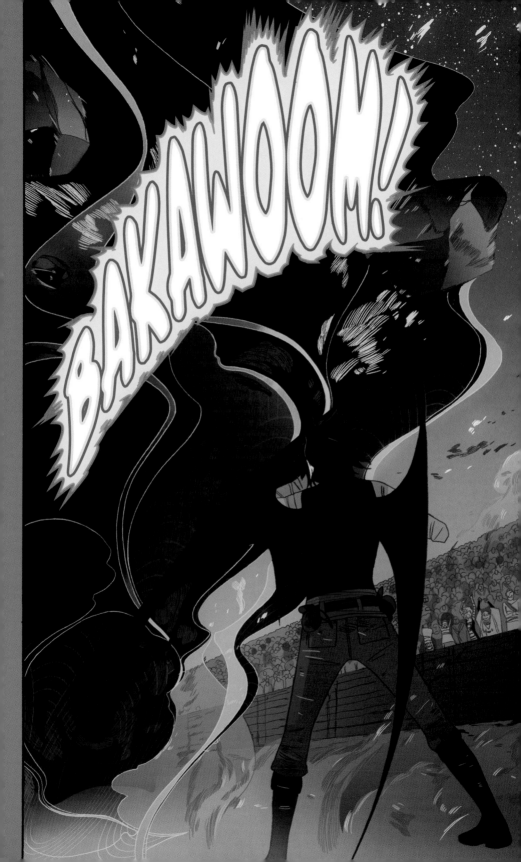

THANK YOU, MY PRINCE! I WILL NEVER FORGET THIS! I'LL DECLARE A FEAST NIGHT IN YOUR HONOR IN THE VILLAGE OF SCARSDEEP!

UUH . . . SURE. NO PROBLEM. HAPPY TO HELP.

WOOO!

HE'S OUR PRINCE!

YEAH!

WHY NOT GIVE THEM A WAVE? IT'S YOU THEY'VE COME TO SEE. WHAT YOU'VE DONE HAS WON THE HEARTS OF OUR PEOPLE MORE COMPLETELY THAN A DOZEN TAX CUTS OR A HUNDRED VICTORIES ON THE BATTLEFIELD.

YOU KNOW, THE OLD PRINCE TALON WOULD NEVER HAVE GONE AFTER THAT CHILD.

NOT BAD, SEIFER TOMBCHEWER. NOT BAD AT ALL.

THEY CAME THROUGH THE FRACTURE WITH OVERWHELMING FORCE. WE COULD NOT HOLD THEM, BUT WE MADE THEM PAY **DEARLY** FOR THEIR INCURSION. THEY LOST TWO THOUSAND IN THE CROSSING.

AND THIS IS THE EXTENT OF THE ENTIRE ILLUMA ARMY? FIVE THOUSAND MEN?

PRINCE TALON, THE ILLUMA ARMY NUMBERS FIVE **HUNDRED** THOUSAND. WHAT WE ARE SEEING HERE IS THE VANGUARD. IF THEY CAN SECURE THE FRACTURE, THEY WILL BRING THE OTHERS THROUGH. BUT UNTIL RAVENFELL IS THEIRS, THEY WILL NOT DARE RISK IT.

THEN WHAT'S THE PLAN?

SIMPLE. WE **ATTACK.**

BUT THEY HAVE MORE MEN THAN US.

WITH THE RIGHT STRATEGY AND THE ADVANTAGE OF HIGH GROUND, WE CAN OVERCOME THEIR SUPERIOR NUMBERS.

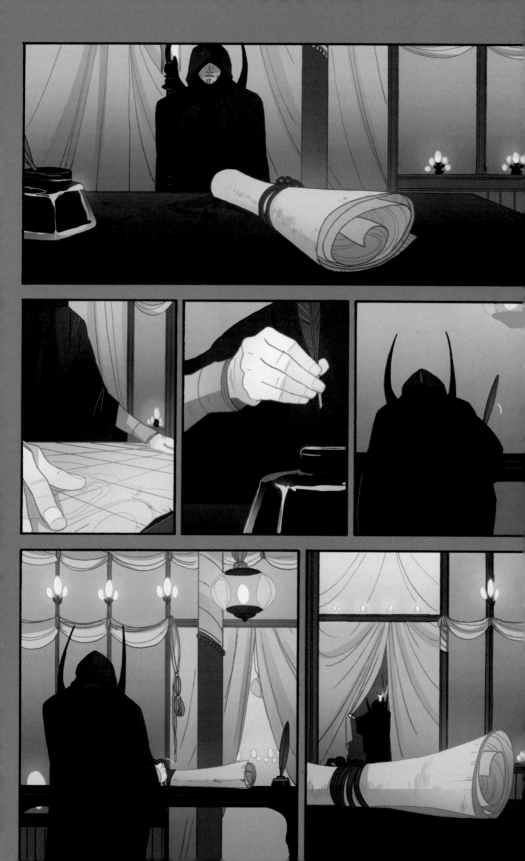

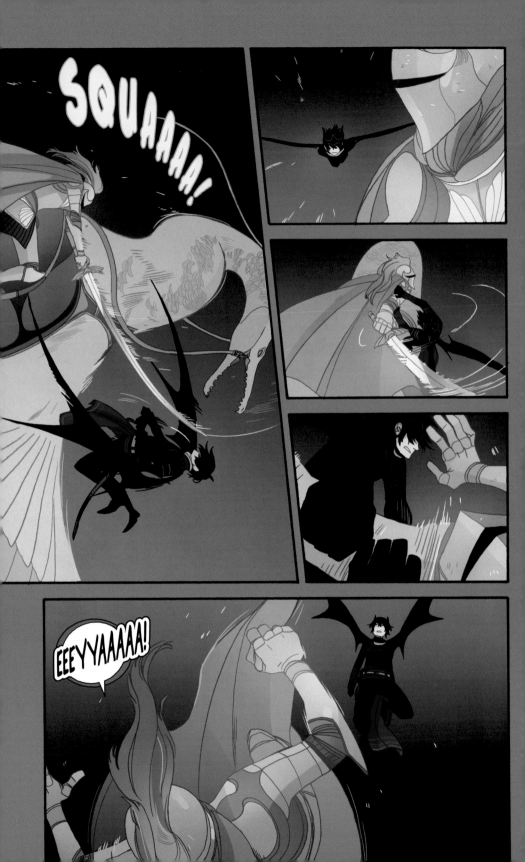

151

153

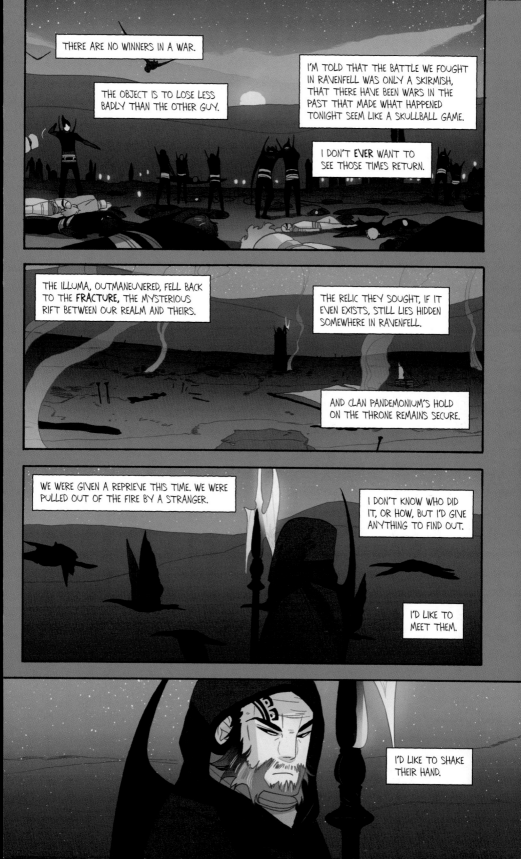

I RETURNED TO A HERO'S WELCOME.

IT SEEMS PRINCE TALON HAS NEVER BEEN SO POPULAR.

YOU KNOW, I COULD GET USED TO THIS.

THE REAL PRINCE IS STILL MISSING, BUT WE'VE FOUND CLUES TO HIS WHEREABOUTS. THE RING THAT THE VELVET SPIES TOOK FROM SNAGGLEFACE, THE WORDS OF THE DEMON ASSASSIN.

THE ILLUMA AND THE OLOGS ARE BOTH INVOLVED. AND THERE'S A TRAITOR IN THE RANKS OF THE DARKLING NOBILITY.

INVESTIGATIONS HAVE BEGUN, BUT WE HAVE TO BE CAREFUL. NOBODY WANTS A WAR WITH THE OLOGS RIGHT NOW.

FINDING PRINCE TALON AND GETTING HIM BACK WILL BE A DELICATE OPERATION.

BUT EVEN LUMBAGO HAS TO ADMIT, I'M DOING A BETTER JOB AS THE PRINCE'S REPLACEMENT THAN ANYONE THOUGHT I WOULD.

SOME PEOPLE PREFER ME TO THE REAL THING.

THOUGH SOME OUT THERE WOULD LIKE TO SEE ME IN THE CEMETERY.

AND SOME JUST CAN'T BE FOOLED.

THE END... FOR NOW